Student Evangelism Training
Guidebook

YOUTH FOR CHRIST

Youth Specialties

ZondervanPublishingHouse

Grand Rapids, Michigan
A Division of Harper Collins *Publishers*

Live the Life! Student Evangelism Training Guidebook

Copyright © 1998 by Youth for Christ/USA

ISBN 0-310-22582-5

Youth Specialties Books, 1224 Greenfield Dr., El Cajon, CA 92021,
are published by Zondervan Publishing House,
5300 Patterson Ave. S.E., Grand Rapids, MI 49530.

Editors: *June Dudley, Todd Temple, and Kaylyn Wilson*
Contributing writers: *Neil Anderson, Byron Emmert, Jim Hancock, Dan Marlow, Josh McDowell,
Jenny Morgan, Bill Muir, Dave Park, Dave Rahn, and Mike Work*
Cover and interior design: *Deborah Razo, Razdezignz*

Printed in the United States of America

98 99 00 01 02 03 / / 10 9 8 7 6 5 4 3

www.livethelife.org
www.youthspecialties.com
www.zondervan.com

SO WHADDAYA SAY?

To your girlfriend?
Boyfriend?
Bestfriend?
Teamfriend?
Parent?

TO SOMEONE WHO NEEDS WHAT YOU HAVE?

Not that you have it all. But at least you feel like you've got Someone along with you, who understands you, who loves you–Someone you can tell *anything* to. And you wish someone you love, or like, or just know, could get to know–or like, or maybe even love–Jesus, like you're learning to.

FIRST YA GOTTA LIVE THE LIFE.

Really, it's simple. You'll use this Guidebook as your youth group journeys through six wild lessons that uncomplicate all this sharing-your-faith stuff. And between lessons you can open up to just about any page and find something interesting. (Go ahead, try it now. We'll wait. And later on, you can even surf to www.livethelife.org to see how other students are figuring this out.)

So claim this Guidebook right now by writing your name on the cover. Then get ready to meet Shannon, Brad, Eva, the Professor–and Jesus Christ, in a way you probably haven't before.

STUFF IN THE FRONT

STUFF IN THE MIDDLE
[THE COURSE]

MORE THAN A NOTEBOOK ——

Quotes from people past and present. Sometimes they're talking about the Christian faith. Sometimes they're talking about something else. But whatever they're talking about, their wise words apply to what *we're* talking about. (Warning: Some of them don't speak English.)

We can't say everything in the lesson. These tips will help you understand key concepts.

STUFF IN THE BACK

Like a notebook, this book has outlines for each of the six lessons, with room for you to write your own notes and ideas. But then it's got a whole lot more: on nearly every page, you'll find helpful tips and food for your mind and heart, including . . .

Maybe you'll hear something in a lesson and think, "What's the big deal? I already know this!" Think again: God just might have something more to say to you on the subject, something deeper. We'll help you dig in and find it.

We've got dozens of video clips to show you. Look for this icon to find out more about a clip—where it comes from, how to apply its message in your own life . . . stuff like that.

WHY I'M LEARNING TO LIVE THE LIFE

Why are you doing this training? Write down three of your top reasons, then circle the one that's most important for you.

UP RULES

They say you shouldn't use the word *rules* with youth group because it sounds so negative. But we don't listen to what "they" say. Besides, these rules are positive—play by them and you'll get the most of your experience. Here they are:

SHOW UP
We've got lots to cover in each session and not a lot of time! So show up . . . in this room . . . on time . . . every time—with your Bible, course guidebook, and pen.

TEAM UP
Stick together, talk together. And while you're at it, SPEAK UP—share from your heart during the Talkbacks and small group discussions.

FESS UP
We're dealing with real life here. So when you speak—in Talkbacks and discussions—tell others what's really going on in your life. Set aside the "Sunday school" perfect answers: be real, or be silent.

GIVE UP
We're not at school! No need to pretend that you know all the answers, that you've got it all together. Instead, admit to yourself and God that you're not perfect . . . you've got things to learn, room to grow, habits to change. Ask God to show you what he's got in store for you each morning.

Seize the Day!

 Grab everything you can each session. Here's how:

Wake up! So you stayed up too late last night. Big deal. Who didn't? But don't let this fact get in God's way. Eat a meal, drink something, run around the block, brush your teeth with anchovy paste . . . whatever it takes to get your eyes, ears, and heart open for these sessions!

Prepare to teach. Nothing makes you learn better than when you know you'll have to teach it to someone else. And you will! In case you haven't noticed, some of your good friends aren't with you. Who's going to show them what you've learned? That's your job . . . if you learn it yourself first. (Hint: Take notes!)

Read between the lines. It took an army of people a whole year to cram these lessons into six short sessions. There's no way you'll catch it all if you just sit back and zone out (like you do when you're watching TV). We've buried cool stuff and deep truths all over the place. Look and listen intently and you'll catch things others miss.

No stray dogs. If you find a stray dog on the street, please don't bring it into the classroom. The howling distracts the youth leader.

GUTSY ACTS

During each session you'll be challenged to apply the lesson message. You have until the next meeting to complete your mission. Then you'll be asked to report on your commitment— how you did, what was tough, and whether or not you're willing to carry through on the commitment even after the training is over.

For each Gutsy Act, you're given four choices:

The first choice is challenging but attainable.

The second choice adds a new hurdle to the first act; it's a bit tougher.

The third choice is very difficult. Do not choose it unless you're willing to set aside your own agenda and lay it all on the line for Jesus that day.

The fourth choice is up to you. If none of the first three choices works for you, or you feel God calling you to a different act, then write it in the lines provided.

You may make different choices on different days. Don't feel that because you committed to the hardest choice for one lesson, you must commit to the most difficult for the next lesson. Choose each act to match your ability and guts.

IMPORTANT: *In many cases, the Gutsy Act you choose demands that you repeat the act for a number of days. Choose wisely—you're making a lasting commitment.*

Thousands of students have been doing Gutsy Acts. Encourage them and challenge yourself at www.livethelife.org

Get a GRIP

To help you with your daily time with God, we have developed a simple framework for you to use. We want you to "get a grip" on spending daily time with God. Use this acrostic for **GRIP** to help you remember and practice these four steps when you spend time with God.

One critical principle you must learn when you are rock climbing is to get a firm grip on the rock. Otherwise, you will never make it up the mountain. So it is with our spiritual life. We must have a firm grip on God's Word to keep us from falling in our daily life.

Get alone with God
(30 seconds)

"Be still, and know that I am God." (Psalm 46:10a) Slow down, open your eyes and ears, and invite God to speak to you.

Read God's Word
(one and a half minutes)

"Do not merely listen to the word, and so deceive yourselves. Do what it says." (James 1:22) Listen to the voice of God! It is how he speaks to us—choose a clear translation like the New Living Translation.

Investigate and respond
(three minutes)

"And remember, it is a message to obey, not just to listen to" (James 1:22-24, *NLT*) Ask, "God—what do I need to become or do today?" Don't read and run! Read and Respond!

Pray about it all!
(two minutes)

"Do not be anxious about anything, but in everything, by prayer and petition, with thanksgiving, present your requests to God." (Philippians 4:6)

Consider writing your prayers—use the simple ACTS acrostic as a guide for the key ways to talk with God:

Adoration—praise God for who he is.
Confession—tell God how you've disobeyed him. Ask for forgiveness.
Thanksgiving—let God know that you're grateful for what he has done in your life.
Supplication—ask God to meet your needs and the needs of other people in your world.

Beginning on page 70 you'll find a week's worth of devotionals to get you started. You can find lots more at www.livethelife.org

SCARED

LET'S ADMIT IT: Sharing your faith with someone can be a pretty frightening experience. Fear of embarrassment, concern that you don't have the right answers, doubts about your own faith—these things can make it pretty tough. We're going to tackle these fears head on!

Take a moment to survey your own fears and concerns. Be honest. What might stand in your way when it comes time to share your faith? Put a checkmark next to the fears and concerns you have. Cross out the ones that aren't a problem for you. And if you have a concern that's not listed, write it in.

CONCERNS ABOUT MY OWN FAITH . . .

○ I'm not sure I'm really a Christian.

○ I don't have a great testimony.

○ I made a commitment to Jesus once, but I don't really live up to it.

○ _____

_____

CONCERNS ABOUT HOW OTHERS SEE ME . . .

○ If others knew what I was really like, they might think I was a fake.

○ My own struggles make it hard to convince others that Jesus makes a difference.

○ I'm afraid I'd lose friends if they knew about my beliefs.

○ _____

_____

CONCERNS ABOUT HOW I TREAT OTHERS . . .

○ I try to love others, but my own selfishness gets in the way.

○ I feel like I'm a hypocrite because I don't do what Jesus says when it comes to serving others.

○ When I try to help people, they often take advantage of me.

○ _____

_____

SILENT

CONCERNS ABOUT SHARING THE GOSPEL MESSAGE ...

○ I want to tell people that they need Jesus, but I'm not sure everyone really does need Jesus.

○ I don't know the right things to say to explain the gospel clearly.

○ If the person started asking me tough questions, I might mess up because I don't have the right answers.

○ If I shared the gospel and the person said yes, I wouldn't know what to do next!

○ I'd probably get nervous and drool or faint or find out later that my zipper was open the whole time.

○ _____

CONCERNS ABOUT MY RELATIONSHIPS WITH OTHER CHRISTIANS ...

○ Few of my friends are Christians. Sometimes I feel like I'm all alone in my beliefs.

○ I don't really have Christian friends who I can be totally honest with.

○ I act one way with my Christian friends, and another way with my other friends.

○ _____

CONCERNS ABOUT MY OWN COURAGE ...

○ When it comes right down to sharing my faith, I'm afraid I might just chicken out!

○ I have so many doubts, I couldn't convince anyone.

○ I tried sharing my faith before, but I messed up.

○ In the past, I've made a commitment to share my faith, but when the excitement of the moment wore off, I kind of gave up on my commitment.

○ _____

Now I'm Really Scared!

Maybe you were feeling pretty good ... until you went over this list and realized all the things you're concerned about. That's okay! You're normal! We didn't create this course for Super-Christians. We designed it for the rest of us—real Christians with real fears, real struggles, real doubts. In each lesson, we'll address the concerns you've checked. Will you be fearless by the end of the training? Nope. But we're confident that you'll be crossing out some of the concerns you've checked. And for the ones that remain ... well, stick around—we've got some good news about that later. Stay tuned.

DEPEND ON JESUS

the Word

And all of us have had that veil removed so
that we can be mirrors that brightly reflect
the glory of the Lord. And as the Spirit of
the Lord works within us, we become more
and more like him and reflect his glory
even more.

2 Corinthians 3:18 (NLT)

¹**Christian** \'krish(h)-chen\ *noun* , _____

_____

_____

_____

_____

_____ <see Christ>

IT'S SIMPLE:

It's not what _____

that makes me a Christian. It's what

_____!

I remember the day my education began. It wasn't the first day of kindergarten. All I

Jesus is my

_____ and

_____.

Real Kids

Sometime ago we "kidnapped" 13 teenagers from all over the country and locked them in a Colorado cabin for the weekend. We asked them tough questions about their life—friends, faith, struggles, and triumphs. They told us—and each other—the truth.

And now, through video, they're telling you.

That took guts on their part. Now it's your turn. Don't just listen to their answers. Listen to your own. Then share your real answers—in this Guidebook, in Talkbacks, with friends, and in your Life Together discussion groups. Now is the time to speak the truth.

JESUS IS MY _____

the Word

But God showed his great love for us by sending Christ to die for us while we were still sinners.

Romans 5:8 (NLT)

When compared to God, each of us is a pretty good example of imperfection: weakness, ignorance, deceit, injustice, mercilessness, and hatred. Not a pretty picture.

It's the only thing we can do: acknowledge Jesus as our savior and rely upon him instead of counting on our own imperfect (and futile) attempts to live life on our own.

Creator of the entire universe; the absolute definition of perfection: strength, wisdom, truth, justice, mercy, and love.

The perfect bridge: His death covers our imperfection so we can stand next to a perfect God. (And BONUS—his resurrection proves that we can live forever with this perfect God.)

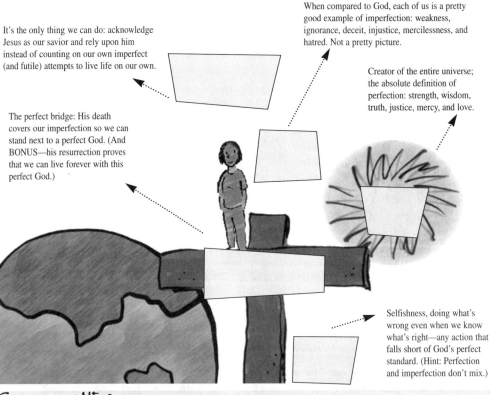

Selfishness, doing what's wrong even when we know what's right—any action that falls short of God's perfect standard. (Hint: Perfection and imperfection don't mix.)

God rescued ME from ...

God rescued ME to ...

rest. And it wasn't my first day in middle school. I managed to keep my pants dry, but

A Personal Savior

You had a reason or circumstance that brought you to the "edge"—to call out to Jesus for rescue. Whatever it was, it showed you your personal need for Jesus. The cool thing is, Jesus rescued you right where you were at. But remember, others may not be at that same place. Their needs are different. Their circumstances are different. And if you want to share the gospel with them, you must find out where they're at. What's their situation? What's going to bring them to the edge?

Do some homework today. Ask your friends what really got them to the edge before they called out for Jesus. Pay attention to their answers. Chances are, you'll run into someone in a similar situation. And you'll know a little bit more about what they might be feeling—and what it is that will help them understand the Good News of Jesus. Jesus wants to rescue them right where they're at. Go there yourself, and you can help light the way.

NIGHT CROSSING

Being a Christian means you've been rescued by Jesus—whether you knew all the dangers or not!

GOD/ME For God so loved the world that he gave his one and only Son, that whoever believes in him shall not perish but have eternal life. John 3:16 *(NIV)*

SIN For all have sinned and fall short of the glory of God. Romans 3:23 *(NIV)*

JESUS For Christ died for sins once for all, the righteous for the unrighteous, to bring you to God. He was put to death in the body but made alive by the Spirit. 1 Peter 3:18 *(NIV)*

TRUST Yet to all who received him, to those who believed in his name, he gave the right to become children of God. John 1:12 *(NIV)*

ended up in a trash can through an ancient ritual carried out by the ruling tribe of

JESUS IS MY _____.

Master, boss, ruler, provider. In this case, you stick some great adjectives in front of the title: kind, loving, merciful, forgiving.

How else but through a broken heart / May Lord Christ enter in? — Oscar Wilde

IT DEPENDS*
I consciously depend on Jesus to help me . . .

always often seldom never

always	often	seldom	never	
❏	❏	❏	❏	Love my parents.
❏	❏	❏	❏	Make moral decisions.
❏	❏	❏	❏	Be a better friend.
❏	❏	❏	❏	Make important choices about my future.
❏	❏	❏	❏	Keep my love life healthy.
❏	❏	❏	❏	Avoid temptation.
❏	❏	❏	❏	Be a good witness to others.
❏	❏	❏	❏	Tell the truth.
❏	❏	❏	❏	Decide how to spend my money.
❏	❏	❏	❏	Control my anger.
❏	❏	❏	❏	Overcome my doubts and fears.
❏	❏	❏	❏	Discipline my thoughts.
❏	❏	❏	❏	Love my parents.

*We use the word here as a verb; as a noun, it refers to an adult diaper, which is an entirely different problem and we won't be discussing it.

the Word

And I pray that Christ will be more and more at home in your hearts as you trust in him.
Ephesians 3:17a (NLV)

"My Heart, Christ's Home"

That's the title of a remarkable little booklet written by Robert Boyd Munger [InterVarsity Press, 1973]. Get a copy! Munger takes you on a heart-house tour that will change the way you see Jesus. And he'll point out a part of the house that we didn't have time to discuss: the hall closet. If you're ready to go deeper, "My Heart, Christ's Home" will show you the way.

eighth graders. My education really began in my junior year of high school. It was a

MY HEART-HOUSE

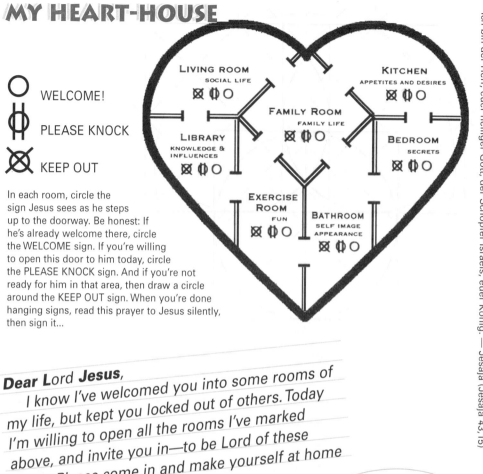

○ WELCOME!

⦶ PLEASE KNOCK

⊠ KEEP OUT

In each room, circle the sign Jesus sees as he steps up to the doorway. Be honest: If he's already welcome there, circle the WELCOME sign. If you're willing to open this door to him today, circle the PLEASE KNOCK sign. And if you're not ready for him in that area, then draw a circle around the KEEP OUT sign. When you're done hanging signs, read this prayer to Jesus silently, then sign it...

LIVING ROOM
SOCIAL LIFE

KITCHEN
APPETITES AND DESIRES

FAMILY ROOM
FAMILY LIFE

LIBRARY
KNOWLEDGE & INFLUENCES

BEDROOM
SECRETS

EXERCISE ROOM
FUN

BATHROOM
SELF IMAGE APPEARANCE

Ich bin der Herr, euer heiliger Gott, der Schöpfer Israels, euer König. — Jesaja (Jesaja 43,15)

Dear Lord Jesus,
I know I've welcomed you into some rooms of my life, but kept you locked out of others. Today I'm willing to open all the rooms I've marked above, and invite you in—to be Lord of these areas. Please come in and make yourself at home in my heart.

Love, _____

Get this: Jesus actually wants to spend time with you! He not only loves you . . . he likes you. Every time you go into a "room" where he's not welcome, you're turning your back on the best friend you ever had. When you invite him to go with you into that area of your life, it's like going on an adventure with your best friend.

Remodel

Maybe in your own heart-house, you associate different life-areas to the rooms. That's okay—just change the floor plan by crossing out words and writing your own room names and life-areas.

QUIET TIME = JESUS TIME

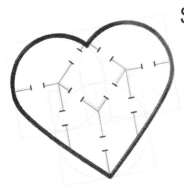

Sin has a way of blowing closed the doors inside our heart. Spending daily quiet time with Jesus is like using a _____ to prop them open.

Getting All You Can from Reading His Word

Here are some ideas you might want to try to take a fresh approach to reading the Bible.

- Read an easy-to-understand Bible like the *New Student Bible (NIV)* or the *New Student's Life Application Bible (NLT)*.
- If a phrase, verse, or passage strikes you, stop and ponder it for a while.
- Rewrite a section in your own words.
- Imagine or picture the scene you're reading about.
- Put yourself in the situation you're reading about and think how you would respond.
- Ask yourself how this applies to you or your situation.
- Read a conversational translation like *The Message*.
- Read as you would any other book or letter.
- Read at different times each day.
- Read a little whenever you have some free time.
- Write a letter back to Jesus in response to what you read.
- Act on anything that God seems to be telling you to do.
- Take one passage and read it in several different translations.

-by Dan Marlow

which my mom said was short for *Jesus*. I never figured out how that worked. Chewy

INTIMACY WITH JESUS—ABIDING IN CHRIST

Who you are is more important than what you do.

Abiding in Christ is being connected to Jesus in a vital, living relationship. In John 15, Jesus teaches the disciples the importance of abiding. He establishes himself as the vine and says that we are to be the branches connected to the vine. Jesus states, "Remain in me, and I will remain in you. No branch can bear fruit by itself; it must remain in the vine. Neither can you bear fruit unless you remain in me. I am the vine; you are the branches. If a man remains in me and I in him, he will bear much fruit; apart from me you can do nothing" (John 15:4-5).

All the activity in the world can't make up for an intimate growing relationship with Jesus. Jesus says that our activity without him is worthless. Abiding in Christ is a lifestyle based on love, trust, and commitment.

A LOOK AT WHAT YOU THINK—QUESTIONS ABOUT ABIDING

◆ Place an X on the continuum of how well you know Jesus.

(Hardly)   **1**   **2**   **3**   **4**   **5**   (Know very well)

◆ How important is your relationship with Jesus?

(Unimportant) **1**   **2**   **3**   **4**   **5**   (Very important)

◆ Looking at how I spend my time, my personal time with Jesus is . . .

(Low priority) **1**   **2**   **3**   **4**   **5**   (High priority)

◆ I trust Jesus with . . .

(Few things) **1**   **2**   **3**   **4**   **5**   (Many things)

FOCUS

There are several ways to maintain an active, intimate relationship with Jesus Christ:

1. SOLITUDE—Setting aside time to be alone with Jesus is vital in developing an intimate relationship with him. We see Jesus' example in Luke 5:16—even he needed to withdraw to a deserted place and pray. We live in a noisy world and it's often hard to discern God's leading in our lives. There are two basic ways God communicates with us. One of the clear ways he speaks to us is through his Word. Another way is prayer, which provides an opportunity for us to speak with him.

2. OBEDIENCE/SURRENDER—One cannot abide in Jesus without obeying his words. John 15:10 says, "If you obey my commands, you will remain in my love, just as I have obeyed my Father's commands and remain in his love." John 14:21 states, "Whoever has my commands and obeys them, he is the one who loves me. He who loves me will be loved by my Father, and I too will love him and show myself to him." The only way we're going to know Jesus and grow in our faith is by obeying his Word out of our love for him.

3. SERVICE—The book *Experiencing God*, by Henry Blackaby and Claude King, states, "It is impossible to be in relationship with God and not have a mission. Our God is always at work around us and invites us to join in his work." Our mission is to serve those around us by communicating Christ to them wherever they are on their journey.

(adapted from *Changing Lives Forever* by Bill Muir. Used by permission of Youth First Communications, copyright ©1997)

was originally from Mexico but had lived next door to my family even before I was

GUTSY ACT #1

DEPEND ON JESUS

Starting today and *every* day this week, I'm committing myself to . . . *(choose one)*

☐ Spend a quiet time with Jesus each day.

☐ Spend a quiet time with Jesus each day . . . *and* commit my full attention during the general church service to worship him.

☐ Spend a quiet time with Jesus each day . . . *and* commit my full attention during the church service to worship him . . . *and* make and keep a prayer journal, setting aside time each day to pray.

☐ *(write your own Gutsy Act)* _____

_____

_____

_____

SIGN HERE as confirmation of your commitment:

_____

Tip: If you don't have a strategy for daily quiet times with God, you can use the Devos starting on page 70 or find a new devotion every day at www.livethelife.org

born. He pronounced Jesus "Hay-SOOS," so it didn't seem that strange to me that he

MEETING 1
LIFE TOGETHER DISCUSSION

Depend on Jesus
Life Together Discussion

1. Why are you taking this Live the Life training? What are you most looking forward to? What are you most afraid of?

2. Refer back to page 14. Finish the following sentences.
   Personally, Jesus rescued me from . . .
   When I decided to trust Jesus . . .

3. Look at page 17. How would you finish the following sentences?
   The room in my life that is most difficult to open up to Jesus is . . . because . . .
   If Jesus were to remodel my heart-house, he would . . .

4. When I think that Jesus wants to spend time with me, I feel . . .

5. Pray together.

had the same name as God's son. Anyway, like so many evenings since I was a little

21

BE REAL

FLASHBACK

The most important thing I learned in the last lesson was

Imperfect Picture

Think of a respected Christian you know very well. If you're really close, you know that he or she isn't perfect. You've seen the flaws, weaknesses, sins. How does this affect your view of the person's faith? Do you question his or her beliefs each time you discover a flaw? Chances are, you understand his or her need for Jesus even more. And you're reminded of your own need for Jesus. Perfect people don't need Jesus. The rest of us do.

kid, this one was spent hanging out on Chewy's porch, talking about sports and

IT'S SIMPLE:

Being a Christian means that I show

you _____

all the time—struggles and all.

WHY BE REAL?

Because you can't convince others that they need

Jesus until you show them that _____.

HOW TO BE REAL: TAKE 3 STEPS . . .

Step 1:_____

Step 2:_____

Step 3:_____

school and stuff. During our chats, he would sometimes test me on my Spanish,

STEP 1:_____.

the Word

Your attitude should be the same that Jesus Christ had. Though he was God, he did not demand and cling to his rights as God. He made himself nothing; he took the humble position of a slave and appeared in human form.

Philippians 2:5-7 (NLT)

--------------------CHARADE OF PERFECTION--------------

PRETENDING THAT MY SIN IS . . .

my own problem.

too small to bother with.

under control.

too big for Jesus to handle.

Perfection

Perfection can mean "without flaw." Few of us have the nerve to claim that we're flawless! But it can also mean "complete, independent, not in need of Jesus' work in our lives." When we pretend perfection in this way, we're doing something very wrong. We need to get humble before Jesus and admit our imperfection.

reading from his Spanish-language newspaper or asking about my day in his native

Dear Jesus,
I know you're perfect, and I'm not, and that I need you to make
me more like you. But sometimes I . . .
• pretend I don't need you;
• assume that my sins are too big for you to forgive;
• figure I'm a pretty good kid with sins too small to bother you;
• exclude you from areas in my life that I'm ashamed of;
• act like I've got to get my life together first, before I come to you
for help.

I know that each of these things is a form of pride. Each time I do
them, I act like I'm in some lofty position—above or beyond your
help. But that's not true. I DO need your help! I can't make it
without you. Please forgive me for my pride. Help me to
remember my need for you.

Love, _____

A Guy Named Jesus

When Jesus showed up on Earth, he didn't just tell us how to live for God. He showed us. Think about it: If he had merely spoken the truth, would people have followed him? His message was believable because he acted it out. We can believe that God is merciful, not merely because Jesus said he is, but because Jesus showed mercy. And we can know that God hates evil . . . not just because Jesus said so, but because Jesus himself got angry at evil.

On your own, take a look at the following verses; each reveals Jesus caught in the act of demonstrating a real human response. Then draw a line from the verse to the emotion or condition it reveals:

Caught in the Act	Human Emotion/Condition
John 11:33-35	Mercy
Matthew 18:32	Disappointment
Matthew 26:40	Joy
Luke 8:47,48	Anger
Matthew 8:10	Forgiveness
Luke 23:42,43	Sadness

Which of the above emotions is most difficult for you to express to others in a godly way? Being real means learning to express your faith through this condition, not in spite of it. Learn to do this in a godly way, and you'll be acting just like Jesus.

Cur ergo haec ipse non facis? — St. Jerome

25

tongue. But this time, he picked up a big black *Biblia* and asked me to translate the

STEP 2: _____.

the Word

For you were once darkness, but now you are light in the Lord. Live as children of light (for the fruit of the light consists in all goodness, righteousness and truth).

Ephesians 5:8-9 (NLT)

OUT OF THE DARK,

INTO THE LIGHT

Problem: Most of us have many layers of darkness obscuring who we really are. Getting out from behind all these layers takes hard work.

Solution: _____.

Layer-Peelers

"Icebreakers" get people talking. Layer-peelers get people to reveal more of who they really are. Try some of these tricks:

"How are you?" When a good friend asks you how you're doing, tell the truth. Then return the question.

Say you're sorry. When you make a mistake or offend someone, admit it. Remorse is a deep emotion—sharing it peels a thick layer.

Confess doubts and fears. Every human has them. When you confess what you're really dealing with, you prove that you're human, too. (Studies show that people prefer to talk to real humans.)

Ask for help. Independence is another thick layer. If a question or problem leaves you stumped, ask a friend. This gesture comes with a bonus: Oftentimes, your friend is honored by your request for help.

words he read: *Oirán pero no entenderán. Verán pero no percibirán.* Apparently it was

THE FIRST LAYER

Peel back the first layer of darkness today! First, write down something that you've been hiding from others—something that you're ashamed of, or haven't been willing to reveal to others because you're afraid of what they'll think. This thing could be a hurt, a doubt, a sin, a fear, an unconfessed wrong. Be honest. (Use code if you want.)

Who are you willing to tell today? (Hint: Pick someone you can trust—a friend or youth leader who can keep your confidence.)

Check here if you're really committed
to peel this layer today: △

Call in an Expert

You don't have to peel alone!

> And all of us have had that veil removed so that we can be mirrors that brightly reflect the glory of the Lord. And as the Spirit of the Lord works within us, we become more and more like him and reflect his glory even more. 2 Corinthians 3:18 *(NLT)*

Did you catch that last line? "... the Spirit of the Lord works within us...." The Holy Spirit works on the inside to help you show people who you really are. Jesus wants you to get out of hiding. Because when you do, others will see him at work inside you! So keep peeling those outside layers in front of people—through honesty, transparency, and confession. And ask the Holy Spirit to keep digging from the inside out.

something the other Jesus had said a long time ago. I struggled through the translation

STEP 3: _____.

We are all in the gutter, but some of us are looking at the stars. — Oscar Wilde

the Word

And find out what pleases the Lord. Have nothing to do with the fruitless deeds of darkness, but rather expose them.
Ephesians 5:I0-II (NIV)

STAYING IN THE LIGHT

As you're peeling back the layers of darkness, you must work hard to stay in the light. Darkness returns quickly!

✧ Get friends who are committed to staying out in the light, too.

✧ Invite close friends to tell you what you need to hear. Give them permission to expose the darkness in your own life.

✧ Become accountable to Christian friends.

✧ Confess to friends your struggles with darkness. (You need their help and prayers.)

✧ Keep short accounts with God. (Don't let layers stack up.)

. . . something like, "They hear but don't understand. They see but don't perceive."

Darkness Repellent

Darkness can creep into our minds through bad and destructive thoughts. For example, hate and hostility cause darkness. What other dark areas can you think of? Satan's lie about darkness is that we have no control over it. Read John 8:44. In Scripture, God reveals the truth through Jesus Christ. In 2 Corinthians 10:3-5, we read that we can conquer these strongholds of darkness. They do not have to control us. Satan's only power over us is what we give him. Our defense against Satan is God's Word, the truth. Read John 8:32 and John 17:15,17. The Bible tells us how to conquer strongholds of darkness:

STEP	SCRIPTURE	SPECIFIC ACTION
1: Renew your mind	Romans 12:2	
2: Prepare your mind for action	1 Peter 1:13	
3: Turn every thought over to God	2 Corinthians 10:5	
4: Pray and turn to God	Philippians 4:6-7	

Here is a brief list of some strongholds of darkness:

Depression	Impure Thoughts	Lust	Inferiority
Gossip	Lying	Hypocrisy	Hatred
Dishonoring Parents	Idolatry	Jealousy	Immorality
Stealing	The Occult	Anger	Unforgiveness
Sexual Sin	Rebellion	Fear	Worry

CIRCLE a stronghold of darkness that you struggle to conquer.

Based on the steps listed above, what specific steps do you need to take to conquer this stronghold of darkness?

1. _____

2. _____

3. _____

4. _____

(adapted from *Busting Free* by Neil Anderson and Dave Park. Used by permission of Gospel Light, ©1997)

Light Reading

"Light" is one of God's favorite self-portraits. Check out these *light* verses:

Romans 13:12	John 1:4-9	Psalm 18:28	2 Corinthians 4:6
John 3:19-20	Psalm 27:1	Ephesians 5:8	John 8:12
Psalm 89:15	John 12:46	Psalm 119:105	Isaiah 2:5
Psalm 119:130	1 John 1:5-7		

But I didn't get the point. Till later. In Spanish class the next morning, the teacher was

NICK'S "BE REAL" JOURNEY

Being real is probably one of the hardest parts of being a Christian. It is so easy just to buy into a personal reality where I am a Christian with no problems. It is almost natural for me to create an image of myself in which I am perfect and not plagued by anything. I have the same temptations that everyone else does—the sex, drugs, and parties are a pressure in all of our lives. We are all tempted at one point or another to lie, cheat, and steal. These are things that I as a Christian have had to face just as anyone else would; the difference is that I am a Christian. People seem to lift Christians up to a high standard, we are expected to be perfect or else we are doing something drastically wrong.

I also feel that if I become real I will be letting God down. Many of the temptations that I do give in to I know are not pleasing to him. This is another reason that I have found it so hard to be a Christian and be real. It wasn't until lately that I discovered the only way to be a Christian in this world is to be real.

As a senior in high school, who's never really been popular, I realized that always trying to look like I never had temptations caught up with me. My best friends would even comment on it. *Hey, Nick, look at that girl . . . oh wait I forgot, you don't have those kinds of feelings* was something I remember hearing quite often, even though I was burning inside. In the process of finally being real this year, I showed a lot of people that I wasn't the uptight Christian I made myself out to be.

People began to see that being a Christian has been an uphill climb for me, and we were able to talk because they could see that I messed up as much as or even more than they did. The thing they needed to see was how I dealt with it when I messed up. They needed to see me put faith in Jesus and trust him to take care of me. Only when I really started doing that and showing people was my faith really effective. My peers saw that Jesus really does take away the sin in my life.

I do have a good many fears about being real. I am afraid that kids will reject me because I don't live up to their standards. I am afraid that I am showing too much of myself to people, that I am letting them too far in. I am afraid of not being perfect. I think about these fears sometimes and I pray. I ask God to take away these fears, and he tells me not to worry. If I am trying my best to live for God, that is what people are gonna see. They will see that I am fallible, but really that is a good thing.

> I AM AFRAID THAT I AM SHOWING TOO MUCH OF MYSELF TO PEOPLE, THAT I AM LETTING THEM TOO FAR IN. I AM AFRAID OF NOT BEING PERFECT.

My friends need to see that God is molding me to be a man in his image and that Christianity is a struggle for everyone involved. That is what I have learned about being real. I need to be real to show people what God can do with someone as dirty as me. I need to be real so that people know they can talk to me because I may have been right where they are at one point, so I may have some answers for them. I also am real because being a Christian is not an act; it is a real part of life. It is a real part of my life and, hopefully, of everyone who comes in contact with me.

—Nick, a high school senior

conjugating the pluperfect of irregular verbs, which had us on the edges of our seats,

WHEN DEALING WITH TOUGH QUESTIONS, REMEMBER . . .

It is normal for your friends to have questions. It is good for your friends to have questions. People ask tough questions for basically two reasons:
1. They are really interested in learning the truth.
2. They are trying to get you off track because they don't want to think or talk about spiritual things.

You don't have to have all the answers to share your faith with your friends. You do need a loving, respectful attitude. (Colossians 4:5-6) You can rely on God's Spirit for confidence and wisdom. (Acts 1:8 and Romans 1:16)

Just be real when you don't know how to answer a tough question— it is OK to tell your non-Christian friend that you don't know the answer, but you'll try to find it.

SOME APPROACHES TO TOUGH QUESTIONS

1. Did Jesus say anything helpful on this topic?
2. Did the other Bible writers discuss the topic at all?
3. Is there anything about the lifestyle of Jesus
   (his character, attitude, actions) that can be applied?
4. What help is there from logic, history, philosophy?

SOME SAMPLE COMMON TOUGH QUESTIONS AND RELATED SCRIPTURE REFERENCES:

1. *Will God really send anyone to hell?*
✪ There is no excuse. (Romans 1:19-21)
✪ Anyone who hasn't accepted Jesus will spend eternity in hell.
   (2 Thessalonians 1:8-9, Matthew 25:46, Revelation 20:15)

2. *What about people in other religions who believe there is more than one way to get to God? Won't God let them into heaven if they are sincere?*
✪ Christianity is unique because of grace. All other religions require the person to earn their way to God through various methods. Jesus claimed that he was God and that belief in him is the only way to eternal life.
   (John 3:3, 15-18; John 10:26-30; John 14:6-9; John 1:12)

3. *How can I know that the Bible is reliable?*
✪ The Bible claims to be a credible historical document.
   (Luke 1:1-4, John 1:1-4, 1 Corinthians 15:1-8, 2 Peter 1:16)
✪ Because we accept Jesus as Lord, we accept his view of the Bible.
   (Matthew 5:17-19, John 14:26)

You can find more help with Tough Questions at www.livethelife.org

as you can imagine. I was thinking about what Chewy had said last night. Then I laughed

GUTSY ACT #2

BE REAL

Today, I'm committing myself to . . . *(choose one)*

☐ Open up, get out, and peel off one layer of darkness, by sharing a hidden fear, doubt, or secret sin with someone I trust.

☐ Share a hidden fear, doubt, or secret sin with someone I trust . . . *and* confess this secret to an adult leader from my group.

☐ Share a hidden fear, doubt, or secret sin with someone I trust . . . *and* confess this secret to an adult leader from my group . . . *and* discard all pretense, "attitude," and selfish pride . . . be real . . . "stay out" . . . let others clearly see Jesus at work in me.

☐ *(write your own Gutsy Act)* _____

_____

_____

_____

SIGN HERE as confirmation of your commitment:

_____

Pretense Busters

If you've made the third choice, you've got your work cut out for you! A few tips:
  • Lose any habitual attitude of arrogance, independence, superiority.
  • Discard your "image"—the polished one you want others to see . . . *including* members of the opposite sex.
• If you're wearing a "Christian" T-shirt or band shirt or anything else that carries a statement, take it off and wear something else today. Let your words and actions speak for you while you carry out this Gutsy Act.
• Admit your errors and offenses immediately.
• Say you're sorry. Ask for forgiveness. If you're unreconciled or angry with someone, settle this account immediately.
• Admit you're scared.
• Throughout the day, repeat this part of 2 Corinthians as a confident reminder of Jesus at work in your heart: "*As the spirit of the Lord works within us, we become more and more like him.*"

32

MEETING 2
LIFE TOGETHER DISCUSSION

How To Be Real in Your LT Group

1. Be honest or be silent.
2. Don't blab outside the group.

Be Real
Life Together Discussion

1. Refer to page 21. Share how you did in your commitments. What was the toughest part? Will you act on these commitments again today?

2. Think of a time when someone you respected opened up to you and revealed a flaw, weakness, or sin in his or her own life. Describe how you felt and how your image of that person changed.

3. It's hard for me to open up and tell friends who I really am because . . .

4. One weakness, fear, or doubt that most people don't know about me is . . .

5. Pray together.

the teacher because I was busy thinking about sitting in class and hearing but not

LOVE OTHERS

But Cristes loore and his apostles twelve / He taughte, but first he folwed it hymselv. — Geoffrey Chaucer (*The Canterbury Tales*)

the Word

Dear friends, I am not writing you a new command but an old one, which you have had since the beginning. This old command is the message you have heard. Yet I am writing you a new command; its truth is seen in him and you, because the darkness is passing and the true light is already shining.

I John 2:7-8 *(NLT)*

FLASHBACK

The most important thing I learned in the last lesson was

the Word

Love your neighbor as yourself.

Luke 10:27b *(NIV)*

IT'S SIMPLE:

Living as a Christian means only two things:

_____,

_____.

understanding. It was one of those barber shop mirror things—a reflection of a

Love God

We just read the second part of Luke 10:27. Here's the first part: He answered: "Love the Lord your God with all your heart and with all your soul and with all your strength and with all your mind."

Luke 10:27a

Sounds a lot like "Depend on Jesus as Lord." If you were to take another trip through your heart (see page 17), which rooms does this verse apply to?

My heart
My soul
My strength

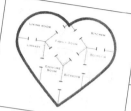

FOUR BIG QUESTIONS

WHY _____ THEM?

WHO'S MY _____?

HOW DO I LOVE _____?

HOW DO I LOVE _____?

Vi elsker fordi Han elskede os først. — 1 John 4:19

Rearrange Your World

You were put on this planet to improve the lives of other people—to help them find more freedom, justice, happiness, health, and purpose by meeting Jesus Christ. When you wake up in the morning, ask yourself, *How can I make life better for the people I meet today? How can I show Jesus' love to others?*

- Tell your parents you love them.
- Smile at a stranger.
- Tell a teacher you think she's doing a good job.
- Treat a cashier or clerk with respect. Say thank you.
- Let a friend know how much you appreciate his friendship.
- Write an encouraging note to someone who's going through a tough time.
- Help your sister do her chores.
- Instead of walking past a pile of litter, pick it up and throw it away.
- Send a postcard to a friend who's moved away.

The simplest gestures—smiles, hugs, handshakes, pats on the back—can help you fulfill your goal. Each says, "I'm happy you're alive." Simple comments— "Please," "Thank you," "Pardon me," "I'm sorry," "I like you," "I love you," "You're a good friend," "You yodel divinely," "How can I help?"—can change someone's day. Each expresses your willingness to put others first.

(adapted from *How to Rearrange Your World* by Todd Temple. Used by permission, ©1992)

reflection of a reflection. Way too deep for first period. Easier to pay attention. For a

WHO'S MY _____?

ANSWER: _____.

JESUS TELLS A STORY

Name of the story:

Summary

Why did Jesus choose a Samaritan as the hero?

"Don't the Bible say we must love everybody?" "Oh, the Bible! To be sure, it says a great many such things; but, then, nobody ever thinks of doing them—you know, Eva, nobody does." — Harriet Beecher Stowe (Uncle Tom's Cabin)

NEIGHBOR LIST

Check all who qualify as neighbors, according to Jesus' definition:

- my friends
- my parents
- my little sister
- the meanest kid in school
- people who hate me
- that guy in my history class who drools a lot
- police
- homosexuals
- filthy rich people
- poor people
- people who love the kind of music I hate
- people on the other side of the planet
- my teachers
- people whose skin color is different than my own
- foreigners
- members of a cult
- people who belong to a different religion

36 minute or so, anyway. Then I started thinking about *why* Chewy had chosen these

QUESTION 2
WHY _____THEM?

ANSWER: _____.

Simply acting like Jesus is the best way to let your friends find out that you're a Christian.

주님의 삶을 살아라

Divine Appointments

Here's a challenge—begin your day by praying for a "divine appointment," a meeting arranged by God for you to take notice of someone else who needs Jesus.

"Jesus please allow me to connect with someone today who is ready to know more about you. Help me to recognize them when we meet and give me boldness to tell them about you. Amen."

Evangeline

Our own Evangeline got her name from Evangeline Booth (1865-1950), daughter of William and Catherine Booth, the founders of The Salvation Army. Eva Booth commanded the Army in the United States and eventually became General worldwide. She was the most influential Christian woman of her time. Eva dedicated her life to loving others boldly in the name of Jesus. If there's a Salvation Army ministry in your town, chances are it was started or expanded while Eva was in command.

HOW DO I LOVE _____?

ANSWER: _____.

DOING WHAT'S BEST

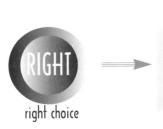

I choose what I think is best for me.

right choice

Even when I make the wrong choice, I do it because I think it's best for me at the moment.

wrong choice

CONCLUSION: WE ALWAYS CHOOSE WHAT WE THINK IS BEST FOR US.

The first duty of love is to listen. — Bill Muir

But Isn't Self-Love Wrong?

Yes, if it's selfishness or arrogance or addiction or boldfaced pride. But basic self-love is not only good, it honors Jesus. Look at it this way: Jesus loved you so much that *he died* to cover the sinful imperfection that would have kept you two apart for *eternity*. Now that's love!

If the smartest, coolest, most wonderful person in the universe loves you, well . . . then you're definitely worth loving! And if you love the same person Jesus loves, he's pretty pleased. That person just happens to be . . . *you.*

but did I *understand* it? How many days had I sat in class, hearing but not

HOW STRONG IS YOUR SELF-LOVE?

It's measured in *perspective*.

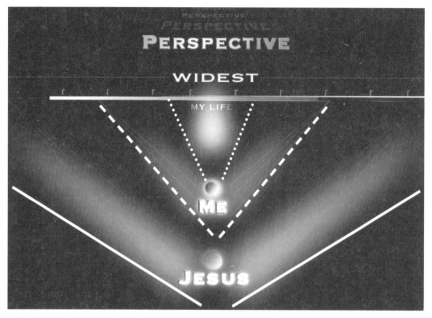

PERSPECTIVE

WIDEST

MY LIFE

ME

JESUS

· · · · · · · · · · · **a little:** what's best right now
− − − − − − **a lot:** what's best in the long run
─────── **ultimate:** what's best eternally

IT'S SIMPLE:

I truly love _____ **each time I do**

what is _____.

A Realistic Model

Ever stop to think about why Jesus chose self-love as the model to love others? What if he had said, "Love your neighbor like your dad loves you"? That would work for some people, but those who don't have a great dad are out of luck. How about, "Love your neighbor like God loves you"? Now that's an impossible standard!

When you look at it that way, you see that Jesus chose a model for love ALL of us can use. If you don't have a lot of self-love, you won't be capable of loving others more. And as your understanding of Jesus and his love grows, your self-love grows, and so too your ability to love others. Jesus is one smart guy.

HOW DO I LOVE _____?

ANSWER: _____.

HOW STRONG IS YOUR LOVE FOR OTHERS?

Again, it's measured in *perspective.*

PERSPECTIVE

LOVE IN PERSPECTIVE

WHEN YOUR FRIEND . . .

	a little love?	more love?	MAXIMUM LOVE (the only real choice)
OFFENDS YOU	punch in the nose *(nicer than a full-blown thrashing)*	ignore *(so she'll learn her lesson)*	forgive *(so she'll see a forgiving Jesus in you)*
ABANDONS YOU	punch in the nose *(you're on a roll)*	abandon him yourself *(a taste of his own medicine)*	stick by him *(so he'll see a relentlessly committed Jesus in you)*
DOES DRUGS	slap in the face *(her nose is sore)*	look the other way *(it's her own life anyway)*	confront her in love *(so she'll see a Jesus who cares enough to risk friendship to save a life)*
GIVES UP ON GOD	smack on the head with a Bible *(God's Word is heavy)*	let him go *(faith is a personal thing)*	pour on the love and prayer *(so he'll see that God hasn't given up on him)*

Jesus tells us to do seemingly impossible things like loving our enemies and praying for those who hurt us. Why? Because he has an eternal perspective: He knows that our love may point these people to himself.

days—starting with that first wet ride to kindergarten. But I was in Spanish class, so I

MY NEIGHBORHOOD, MY WORLD

Take a quick trip into your own world and identify a few key people you know in each box. Write down their names. (Hint: You don't have to write down everyone you know—just two or three key names in each section.)

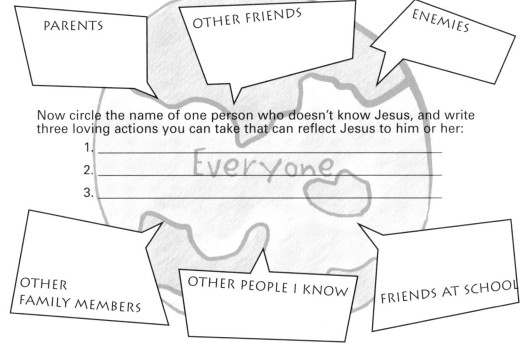

PARENTS

OTHER FRIENDS

ENEMIES

Now circle the name of one person who doesn't know Jesus, and write three loving actions you can take that can reflect Jesus to him or her:

1. _____
2. _____ Everyone _____
3. _____

OTHER FAMILY MEMBERS

OTHER PEOPLE I KNOW

FRIENDS AT SCHOOL

Jesus on Social Etiquette

As the designer of the human race, Jesus has some things to say about how we ought to behave in public. He spelled out a few in a sermon on a mountain top:

• **You are the light of the world—like a city on a mountain, glowing in the night for all to see.** Don't hide your light under a basket! Instead, put it on a stand and let it shine for all. In the same way, let your good deeds shine out for all to see, so that everyone will praise your heavenly Father. Matthew 5:14-16 *(NLT)*

• **You have heard that the law of Moses says 'Love your neighbor' and hate your enemy.** But I say, love your enemies! Pray for those who persecute you! . . . If you are kind only to your friends, how are you different from anyone else? Even pagans do that. But you are to be perfect, even as your Father in heaven is perfect. Matthew 5:43-48 *(NLT)*

• **Take care!** Don't do your good deeds publicly, to be admired, because then you will lose the reward from your Father in heaven . . . Give your gifts in secret, and your Father, who knows all secrets, will reward you. Matthew 6:1-4 *(NLT)*

• **If you forgive those who sin against you, your heavenly Father will forgive you.** But if you refuse to forgive others, your Father will not forgive your sins. Matthew 6:14-15 *(NLT)*

• **Stop judging others and you will not be judged.** Matthew 7:1 *(NLT)*

just thought of the three years I had spent studying a language I still couldn't speak.

HOW DO NON-CHRISTIANS SEE ME?

A great question to ponder: "How does the way I view myself match
how my non-Christian friends and family see me?"

I SEE ME AS . . . lunchroom evangelist	**MY FRIENDS SEE ME AS . . .** the person who mooches lunch money
I SEE ME AS . . . sports evangelist	**MY TEAMMATES SEE ME AS . . .** the person who wins at any cost
I SEE ME AS . . . wonderchild	**MY PARENTS SEE ME AS . . .** the child who has to be asked 12 times to . . . pick up my room, take out the trash, help out around the house, whatever
I SEE ME AS . . . intellectual evangelist	**MY TEACHERS SEE ME AS . . .** the person who knows it all— all the time—about everything
I SEE ME AS . . . dating evangelist	**MY DATES SEE ME AS . . .** the person who treated them as no different than anyone else

Now, try some of your own:

I SEE ME AS . . .   MY FRIENDS SEE ME AS . . .

I SEE ME AS . . .   MY PARENTS SEE ME AS . . .

I SEE ME AS . . .   MY TEAMMATES SEE ME AS . . .

I SEE ME AS . . .   MY DATES SEE ME AS . . .

_____ SEE ME AS . . .

I SEE ME AS . . .

Message missed. And I thought of all the other messages, in and out of school, that

ARE THEY READY? HOW CLOSE ARE YOU?

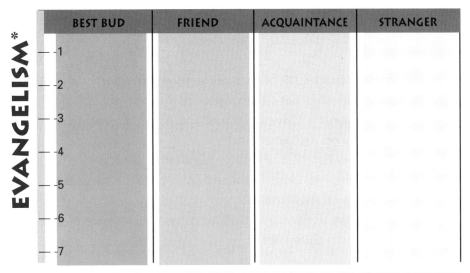

EVANGELISM*	BEST BUD	FRIEND	ACQUAINTANCE	STRANGER
-1				
-2				
-3				
-4				
-5				
-6				
-7				

*EVANGELISM LEGEND

[-1] **NO OTHER CHOICE**
"I've decided to ask Jesus to be my Lord (run my life) and Savior (deal with my own sin problem)."

[-2] **NO OTHER HOPE**
"I can see areas of my own life that convice me that I need Jesus Christ as my Lord and Savior."

[-3] **NO NEGATIVES**
"I think that it would be a good thing for me to commit my life to Jesus Christ."

[-4] **NO EXCUSE**
"I realize that unless I personally ask Jesus Christ to be my Savior and Lord, my sin will keep me separated from God."

[-5] **NO PERSONAL STAKE**
"I believe that Jesus Christ died on the cross so that the whole world could go to heaven."

[-6] **NO UNDERSTANDING**
"I've heard some things about Jesus and the cross, but never figured it out."

[-7] **NO CLUE**
"There may be a God, but I don't know . . . or care."

HOW TO USE THE READINESS/CLOSENESS GRAPH

1. Think of one person who is in your own sphere of influence.

2. Identify what sort of relationship you have with that person. Locate the word at the top of the chart that most accurately describes that relationship.

3. Identify where that person is in his or her own relationship with God. Choose a description from the evangelism legend under the chart. Locate
the correlating number on the left side of the chart.

4. Draw a line from the number on the left to the center of the column that describes your friend. Make an X there.

5. Repeat this process for two other people in your sphere of influence.

MINISTRY STRATEGY

Realize that the farther you are from the left side the more you ought to concentrate on prayerfully living a life that communicates Jesus. As you move closer to the top, more of an emphasis should be placed on prayerfully communicating the words (telling, challenging, encouraging, teaching . . .) about Jesus.

had passed *right through me*. All the things I'd seen and heard—in school, at home, in

GUTSY ACT #3

Today, I'm committing myself to . . . *(choose one)*

☐ Commit a *sacrificial* act of service for another person . . .*
☐ Commit a *sacrificial* act of service for another person . . .**
and tell my parents I love them and appreciate the sacrifices they've made on my behalf . . .**

☐ Commit a *sacrificial* act of service for another person . . .**
and tell my parents I love them and appreciate the sacrifices they've made on my behalf . . .**
and commit my *entire* day to the loving, sacrificial service of others.

☐ *(write your own Gutsy Act)*_____
_____
_____
_____

SIGN HERE *as confirmation of your commitment:*

_____

*Watch carefully for God to show you who, what, and when to do this service!
**I will tell them today by_____(time).

Loving Servant

If you've committed to the third choice, prepare yourself for a very strange day:
• Set aside your own agenda. If you had your own plans for the day, lay them aside and let others decide what they want to do.
• Clean your room. Make your brother's bed. Clean your parent's bathroom. Walk the dog
• Buy lunch for a homeless person. (It's better than giving money.)
• Give up your seat, your place in line—any superior position you have.
• Ask your friends how you can serve them . . . then do it.
• Pray for your teachers, your church leaders, classmates—not just close friends—who are in a hard place.

church, among my friends—what did I miss? What was the point of *any* learning,

MEETING 3
LIFE TOGETHER DISCUSSION

How to Love Others in Your LT Group

As you listen, remember that Jesus has an eternal perspective on each person's life.

- What does Jesus want for this person?
- How can you help make that happen?
- How can you pray effectively for this person?
- And how are you doing in your commitment to love others outside the LT group?

Love Others
Life Together Discussion

1. Refer to page 33. Share how you did in your commitments. What was the toughest part? Will you act on these commitments again today?

2. Look back to page 41. Tell the group about three "neighbors" in your life who you want to learn to love.

3. One person in my life who has demonstrated the love of Jesus is . . . when they . . .

4. One decision that I made recently that reflects self-love—doing what is best for me—not selfish love is . . .

5. What could you do to love each of the neighbors you shared about in question 2?
   - One thing I could do for them that would be best for them eternally is . . .
   - One thing I could do for them that would demonstrate Jesus and his love for them is . . .

6. Pray together.

Share the Gospel

the Word

And all of us have had that veil removed so that we can be mirrors that brightly reflect the glory of the Lord. And as the Spirit of the Lord works within us, we become more and more like him and reflect his glory even more.

2 Corinthians 3:18 (NLT)

FLASHBACK

The most important thing I learned in the last lesson was

IT'S SIMPLE:

Sharing the gospel is simply explaining why the _____ is _____.

It's Good News for _____!

News

The word *evangelism* means "good news." The mystery of the gospel is that it's able to bring good news to our deepest longings and needs. In evangelism, our job is not to convince or convict, but to witness— telling others what we know. This is a great opportunity to show to the world God's mercy, grace, and love.

Chewy was always sneaking God into our porch chats. Many times he told me,

IT'S ALL EVANGELISM

DEPEND ON JESUS
Because if you don't depend on Jesus as Savior and Lord, there's no point in trying to convince others that they need Jesus. Evangelism starts in your own heart.

BE REAL
If you pretend that you're perfect . . . or that your sins don't require Jesus' forgiveness, no one is going to believe your message. First show others who you really are. Then you can talk about how you really need Jesus.

LOVE OTHERS
Your love reveals Jesus to others before you ever open your mouth. You are evidence of a loving Jesus. Display this evidence prominently. Earn the right to be heard.

Isn't There More Than One Way to God?

People often ask, "What's so special about Jesus? Why is he the only way that someone can know God?" Christians are accused of being narrow-minded because we assert there is no other way to get to God. We did not invent the idea of Jesus being the only way. We are merely relating his claim and the claim of the writers of the New Testament.

Jesus answered, "I am the way and the truth and the life. No one comes to the Father except through me" (John 14:6). Paul said, "For there is one God and one mediator between God and men, the man Christ Jesus" (1 Timothy 2:5). It is the testimony throughout the New Testament that no one can know God the Father except through the person of Jesus Christ. Additional verses to look up: John 8:24, Acts 4:12, and 2 Corinthians 5:19, 21.

To understand this, we must go back to the beginning. An infinite, personal God created the heavens, and the earth (Genesis 1:1), and he created people in his own image (Genesis 1:26). Man and woman were placed in a perfect environment, with all their needs taken care of. They were given only one prohibition; they were not to eat of the fruit of the tree of the knowledge of good and evil, lest they die (Genesis 2:17).

Unfortunately, they did eat from the tree (Genesis 3), and the relationship between God and mankind was now broken. However, God promised that he would send a Savior, or Messiah, who would deliver all people from the bondage of sin (Genesis 3:15). The Old Testament kept repeating the theme that some day this person would come into the world and set mankind free.

God's Word did indeed come true. God became man in the person of Jesus Christ (John 1:14, 29). Jesus died in our place so that we could enjoy again a right relationship with God. Jesus has paved the way! God has done it all, and our responsibility is to accept that fact. We can do nothing to add to the work of Jesus; all of it has been done for us. If mankind could have reached God any other way, Jesus would not have had to die. His death verifies the fact that there is no other way. Therefore, no other religion or religious leader can bring someone to the knowledge of the one true God.

At this point many people ask, "Why couldn't God just forgive?" People fail to realize that wherever there is forgiveness, there's also a payment. For example, let's say my daughter breaks a lamp in my home. I'm a loving and forgiving father, so I put her on my lap, and I hug her and I say, "Don't cry, honey. Daddy loves you and forgives you."

Now usually the person I tell that story to says, "Well, that's what God ought to do." Then I ask the question, "Who pays for the lamp?" The fact is, I do. There's always a price in forgiveness. This is what God has done. God has said, "I forgive you," but he was willing to pay the price himself through the cross.

(adapted from A Ready Defense by Josh McDowell. Used by permission of Thomas Nelson Publishers, ©1993)

"Miguel, God has plans for you." If Chewy was right—if God had a reason for my life,

SHARE WHY IT'S GOOD NEWS FOR _____!

My Rescue Story

Once upon a time, _____

Your story should include:
- Where you were at before you met Jesus (Look back to page 14)
- What made you call out to be rescued
- What changed, if anything, as soon as you were rescued
- Why it's still good news for you now

The Real Story

Your rescue story is a *real* story! Don't make it a fiction piece by adding or exaggerating what really happened. Tell the truth—being rescued by Jesus for eternity is plenty exciting, even if it happened in an unspectacular way. Tell others your rescue story at www.livethelife.org

a purpose for my being alive, a mission for me to accomplish—then maybe all this

My Rescue Picture

learning played a part in God's plan. And if *that* were true, then maybe God had plans

ASK: IS THE GOOD NEWS FOR _____?

Ask: If this were a picture of your life . . .

> Where are you?
> What separates you from God?
> What keeps you from having a close relationship with him?
> Does anything else I've said relate in your own life?

Then ask if they want to trust Jesus as their savior.

WHEN THE ANSWER IS _____

DEPEND ON JESUS   BE REAL   LOVE OTHERS

the Word

So neither he who plants nor he who waters is anything, but only God, who makes things grow. The man who plants and the man who waters have one purpose, and each will be rewarded according to his own labor.
I Corinthians 3:7-8 (NLT)

WHEN THE ANSWER IS _____

1. Affirm the person's answer.
2. Ask: "What keeps you from saying yes?"
3. Invite the person to a place where he or she will hear the gospel.
4. Pray!

WHEN THE ANSWER IS _____!

1. Pray together.
2. Ask the person to tell someone else about his or her commitment.
3. Follow up with a phone call.
4. Invite the person to church.
5. Pray regularly for this new Christian!

to *use* my knowledge of Spanish—and history and English and everything else—to

Give me the young man who has brains enough to make a fool of himself! — Robert Louis Stevenson

Rescue Prayer Tips

When someone understands
1. God's story
2. their own need to be rescued
3. the cost of following Jesus

and is ready to ask Jesus to rescue them, it is time for you to lead them in a Rescue Prayer.

Ask your friend to explain to you what it is they want to do. Then say that it is time to tell God the same thing.

While there are no magic words that must be said, it is often more comfortable for your friend to repeat a prayer with you. You can say a phrase, then your friend can repeat it.

Here's a sample Rescue Prayer. Use it or your own words.

> Dear God, I know that my sin has separated me from you. Thank you that Jesus Christ died in my place and rose again to be my Savior. I turn from my sin and trust Jesus to forgive me. Come into my life and lead me. Thank you for giving me a relationship with you forever. In Jesus' name, Amen.

First Steps

1. Make sure your friend understands what happened.
   • Ask your friend what he or she has just done.
   • Ask if Jesus came into his or her life. (If your friend doesn't know or is unsure, then review the Scripture you read and what your friend said to God. Ask your friend what 1 John 5:11-13 says a believer has. Review John 3:16 and ask your friend if he or she has forgiveness and eternal life.)

2. Make sure your friend understands his or her need for spiritual growth.
   • Talk about ways he or she can grow spiritually.
   • Get together within the next two days to pray and read the Bible.
   • Invite your friend to attend church with you.

Newborn Christians are as vulnerable as newborn babies. — Bill Muir

change the world in some way. If God were even half as wise and wily as my old

FOLLOW UP

1. BIBLE

The Bible is an essential source of nourishment to the new believer.

- Within one day of your friend accepting Jesus, give him or her a Bible to provide this important source of nourishment (an easy-to-understand translation). Together, in the front of the Bible, write in the date of your friend's "spiritual birthday"—the date he or she trusted Christ.

- Show your friend how the Bible works—explain that the Bible is like a letter from God to us. Help your friend understand how the Bible is organized— book, chapter, verse. Read some of your favorite verses together and talk about what they mean to you. Suggest some passages to read before the next time the two of you meet, such as the first two chapters of Mark or Psalm 103.

2. STAY IN TOUCH

There are a lot of things your friend needs to talk about. Here is a timetable for getting together.

24 HOURS—Call to find out how your friend is feeling about trusting Jesus.

THREE DAYS LATER—Meet with your friend after school or for lunch. Review the new believer's decision to follow Christ. Ask how he or she feels about this decision. Look at 2 Corinthians 5:17, 1 John 5:11-13, John 1:12, Colossians 1:21. Allow the new believer to ask as many questions as he or she would like. If you don't have all the answers, find them or talk to someone else, like a youth leader or pastor.
- Pray together.
- Set an appointment for the next week.
- Give an assignment to read, Mark 1-3 or Romans 12. Encourage your friend to write down questions he or she has while reading the Bible.

neighbor, that's exactly what he would do. What's more, maybe the words I heard and

STRATEGY

A WEEK LATER—Ask the new believer how the week went. Ask if he or she has any questions about Mark 1-3. Find out if your friend has any doubts about his or her decision to follow Christ. Give the new believer a copy of *Totally True* (available through Youth for Christ, 1-800-735-3525) and start the first chapter together.
- Pray together.
- Invite your friend to church.
- Give the assignment to finish the first chapter and start the second chapter of *Totally True*.

DURING THE NEXT FIVE WEEKS—Meet with your friend weekly and study another chapter from *Totally True*. Make sure you leave enough time to pray together about issues and concerns in your friend's life. In your times together, ask about how your friend's church experience has been so far.

3. CHURCH

Church is a vital and essential part of every believer's life.

Hebrews 10:25 states, "Let us not give up meeting together, as some are in the habit of doing, but let us encourage one another—and all the more as you see the Day approaching." In Ephesians 4:12-14, Paul states that the church is where each of us is equipped for the work of the ministry.

Encourage new believers to:
- Go to church regularly and sit in the first three rows.
- Attend a Bible study at church or youth group to get to know other Christian teens.

If possible, take new believers to church with you:
- Encourage them to take their Bible with them to church.
- Encourage them to take notes on the sermon and lesson.
- Encourage your youth pastor to meet and establish a relationship with new believers.
- Have your youth leader invite the new believer to an upcoming Bible study or youth event.

(adapted from *Changing Lives Forever* by Bill Muir. Used by permission of Youth First Communication, ©1997)

GUTSY ACT #4

SHARE THE GOSPEL

Today, I'm committing myself to . . . *(choose one)*

☐ Share the gospel with a friend.

☐ Share the gospel with a friend . . .
and write a one-page account of my rescue story today, imagining
that this person would read it. *(Don't send the note—it's just
practice for you . . . when you share, you'll want to do it face to face.)*

☐ Share the gospel with a friend . . .
and write a one-page account of my rescue story today,
imagining that this person would read it . . .
and read your rescue story to someone else.

☐ *(write your own Gutsy Act)* _____

_____

_____

_____

_____

SIGN HERE *as confirmation of your commitment:*

_____

. . . sent to *my* ears, *my* eyes—so that I would understand *my* mission. That changed

MEETING 4
LIFE TOGETHER DISCUSSION

Share the Gospel
Life Together Discussion

1. Refer to page 45. Share how you did in your commitments. What was the toughest part? Will you act on these commitments again today?

2. One time I shared my rescue story with someone and . . .

3. My biggest fear when I consider talking about Jesus is . . .

4. In the last lesson we each identified three neighbors. What would it take for you to be able to share your rescue story with one of your three neighbors?

5. Break into pairs and share your rescue story with your partner. After three to five minutes, switch roles.

6. How did it feel to tell your story to someone else? How did you feel when you heard your partner's story?

7. Pray together.

everything. Suddenly, learning—*all* learning—wasn't about grades, or getting into

55

GET CONNECTED

the Word

And let us consider how we may spur one another on toward love and good deeds. Let us not give up meeting together, as some are in the habit of doing, but let us encourage one another—and all the more as you see the Day approaching.

Hebrews 10:24-25 *(NLT)*

FLASHBACK

The most important thing I learned in the last lesson was

IT'S SIMPLE:

To be a Christian is to live together in the

_____.

Carry each other's burdens, and in this way you will fulfill the law of Christ.

Galatians 6:2 *(NIV)*

GET CONNECTED IN THREE STEPS:

STEP 1: Get _____.

STEP 2: Find a _____.

STEP 3: Live _____.

college, or impressing my Sunday school teacher. It was about training for my

STEP 1: GET _____.

WHO SHOULD BE ON THE TEAM
Friends who . . .
- can be trusted
- share your commitment to Jesus
- can be real with each other
- aren't afraid to hold you accountable
- can commit to a weekly time together
- are all the same sex as you

WHEN TO MEET
Pick a weekly time, day, and place that everyone on the team can commit to:
- before school
- at lunch
- before youth group or club meeting
- during morning break
- after school
- after church

TEAM PROSPECTS
Write the names of potential team members. Then circle the names of the most likely candidates.

_____   _____

_____   _____

_____   _____

_____   _____

Why Not a Coed Team?

Girls and guys on the same team—why not? It's not really a romance thing . . . and it's certainly not a sex thing. The fact is, guys tend to share more honestly and openly about themselves among other close male friends. Same thing for girls. Forming a team with members of your gender will most likely result in deeper, safer, more fruitful discussions. And if you're one of those exceptional people who get along better with the opposite sex, you need to be in a same-gender group so you can teach your friends how to deepen their opposite-sex friendships!

mission from God. *What* mission? I didn't know what it was at the time. But I was

57

STEP 2: FIND A _____.

WHAT TO LOOK FOR IN A COACH

You're not asking for a big time commitment here. The coach doesn't have to meet with your team. But every week or so, your coach should be able to ask you how you're doing, find out if there are any issues that need his or her help, and hold your team accountable to your commitment to meet together.

QUALIFICATIONS:
- a strong Christian adult
- respected by your teammates
- same sex as your team
- will take the time to check up on you, hold you accountable

CONSIDER THESE PEOPLE:
- youth director or club leader
- youth group or club volunteer
- pastor
- Christian teacher
- older Christian friend

COACH PROSPECTS:
Write the names of potential team coaches. Then circle the name of the most likely candidate.

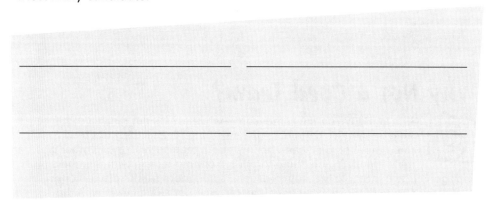

To hoverder er bedre end et.

pretty sure that I'd discover it as I learned. So that day, I began to understand what Jesus

STEP 3: LIVE _____.

TOGETHER: Share who you really are, struggles and all. Share from your heart, confess, talk about your spiritual walk.

TOGETHER: Share how you're doing in your relationships—family, friends, boyfriend or girlfriend, others in your world. Most important, talk about how you're sharing the gospel with those around you!

TOGETHER: Pray together, read the Bible together, worship together.

Successful LT Teams

When team members feel accepted, loved, and understood, they will talk more, reveal more, and learn more. The better the relationships between members, the better the energy, learning, conversation, and interaction between them. Here are some ways to develop trusting friendships in an LT team:

Create a safe place for each Life Together member to share options and experiences by having these three rules:
   1. Be honest when talking or be silent.
   2. Everything shared in the group is confidential.
   3. Everyone commits to attending the LT team meetings. The initial commitment can be for 4 to 8 weeks, with the option to recommit after that time. These three rules help build trust and cohesiveness between team members.

Share leadership. Decide who is going to be your group's leader. You may pick one person to do it all the time or you may rotate so that a different person is responsible each week.

Start slowly. Don't be in a hurry. Developing openness among the team members will take time. Plan activities and games that will help members get to know each other.

Work on a project together. When people work on a common task, they naturally feel closer to each other. Some project ideas are: painting an elderly person's home, helping with yard work, visiting a convalescent home, or helping in your church's nursery.

Build a caring atmosphere. You begin this by showing concern and respect for each other and by listening and accepting the other members of your team.

(adapted from *Changing Lives Forever* by Bill Muir. Used by permission of Youth First Communication, ©1997)

had said. Both of them. I decided to look and listen. With eyes and ears wide open.

LIFE TOGETHER COVENANT

Once you have your LT team organized, here is a plan that you can follow in your weekly meetings. Distribute a copy of Challenge 2001 to every member of your LT team. If you want to commit yourself to following this challenge, sign the covenant.

Each week when your LT team meets, use one of the challenges as your focus for accountability. The first week, talk about your commitment to your relationship with Jesus; the second week talk about how, or if, Christ is active in your moral life, and so on. At the end of six weeks, start over again at the top of the list.

CHALLENGE 2001

Because Jesus Christ loves me and I love him, I will:

Commit—myself to a love relationship with Jesus Christ . . . through praying, studying his Word, and allowing his Spirit to lead me each day. Matthew 22:36-38

Honor—Christ in my moral life . . . my thoughts, words, actions, and relationships. 1 Timothy 4:12

Respect—my parents and all authorities in my life . . . with love, honor, and obedience. Ephesians 6:1-3, Romans 13:1

Involve—myself in encouraging and uniting with other Christians . . . regardless of race, church, or social status. Hebrews 10:24-25

Seek—God through prayer . . . asking him daily to bring spiritual awakening to my generation. 2 Chronicles 7:14

Take—the message of Christ to my school and world . . . by praying, living, and witnessing so that every student has the opportunity to know Christ. Acts 1:8

THE COVENANT

Believing God has a special destiny and mission for me and my generation, I take this challenge, relying on the Holy Spirit.

I join young people and youth workers around the world to pray for a spiritual awakening and to help take the message of Christ to every school and every young person by the year 2001.

_____

Signature

Teamwork divides the task and doubles the success. — Bill Muir

Because if I did have a mission, I was going to be prepared to fulfill it. Message caught. —

THE CHURCH

A log in a fire burns brightly as long as it stays in the fire. But if the log is removed from other logs, it begins to smolder and burn out. In the same way, we need to worship and meet together so we don't end up just blowing smoke.

The church is not a building, but a community of believers. Groups of believers can meet in a building that we normally call a church, but they can also meet in a home, park, or somewhere else. It's important that you meet regularly with other Christians because there are certain things you need from the Church and other things the Church needs from you.

Church Tips

1. Sit in one of the first three rows at church.
2. Always take notes of the sermon or talk.
3. Say something encouraging to someone else while you are there.
4. Take your Bible with you.

---

1. Which of the following do you think are reasons to attend church?

◇ I need to get recharged to face life's difficulties.

◇ I need to be taught God's Word.

◇ I need to worship God.

◇ There's a cute guy or girl there.

◇ I need fellowship with other Christians.

◇ I meet interesting people in church.

2. Which statements describe your attitude now concerning church?

◇ I'm bored.

◇ I hate the songs.

◇ I'm critical.

◇ I go through the motions.

◇ I'm attentive.

◇ My mind wanders.

◇ I'm focused on God.

◇ I'm enthusiastic.

◇ I wish I had a book to read.

◇ I look at my watch.

REMEMBER that the Church isn't a building. It's a body—Jesus' body on earth. We are his hands, his feet, his legs, his mouth. A healthy church will provide you opportunities to share your gifts and be of service to others.

(adapted from *Totally True* by Bill Muir. Used by permission of Fast Forward, ©1991)

Michael Trubble

GUTSY ACT #5

GET CONNECTED

Today, I'm committing myself to . . . *(choose one)*

☐ Go through my list of potential team members* and pray for each of them by name today.

☐ Go through my list of potential team members* and pray for each of them by name today . . .
and share my team plans with an adult friend.

☐ Go through my list of potential team members* and pray for each of them by name today . . .
and share my team plans with an adult friend . . .
and talk with each of these team members in person or by phone, to invite them to join with me and to schedule our first "team time."

☐ *(write your own Gutsy Act)* _____

_____

_____

_____

SIGN HERE *as confirmation of your commitment:*

_____

*See page 49 for your list of team prospects.

Being Real with My Team

A temptation I face is to be real with someone once and then walk back into my solitude. However, being real requires walking the entire journey, not just a couple steps. It isn't enough to be real once to help myself feel better and then walk my own way. To stay real is to put myself in this peculiar place of extreme vulnerability each moment. I must remember that my ability to be real with others stems from my ability to be real with myself and God.

Ecclesiastes 4:10 speaks of the benefits of being real with someone: "If one falls down, his friend can help him up. But pity the man who falls and has no one to help him up!" With my fear of being real, I didn't want anyone to know if I fell. However this left me with no one to lift me up. I found myself alone. But when I am connected with someone else, that friend is there to lift me up. That is the true security of being real.

—Justin, a high school senior

MEETING 5
LIFE TOGETHER DISCUSSION

How to Get Connected in Your LT Group

Remember and practice the three agenda items of a LT team meeting:

Be real together
Love others together
Depend on Jesus together

Get Connected
Life Together Discussion

1. Refer to page 55. Share how you did in your commitments. What was the toughest part? Will you act on these commitments again today?

2. Finish these sentences.
   • When I think about forming a Life Together team with others,   I feel . . .
   • The best part about having this kind of accountability with others is . . .
   • The most difficult part about having this kind of accountability with others is . . .
   • I do/do not want to have a Life Together team because . . .

3. Who would you like to be on your team? Who would you like to have as your adult coach? When, specifically, can you talk to each of these people?

4. Pray together.

HAVE COURAGE

the Word

I have told you these things, so that in me you may have peace. In this world you will have trouble. But take heart! I have overcome the world.

John 16:33 (NIV)

FLASHBACK

The most important thing I learned in the last lesson was

IT'S SIMPLE: Courage means acting as if

my _____ is bigger than

my _____.

SCARED _____ SILENT

What fears and concerns have you overcome this week?
What remains to be conquered?

God on Fear

I sought the LORD, and he answered me; he delivered me from all my fears.
Psalm 34:4

God is our refuge and strength, an ever-present help in trouble.
Psalm 46:1

Peace I leave with you; my peace I give you. I do not give to you as the world gives. Do not let your hearts be troubled and do not be afraid.
John 14:27

The LORD himself goes before you and will be with you; he will never leave you nor forsake you. Do not be afraid; do not be discouraged.
Deuteronomy 31:8

So do not fear, for I am with you; do not be dismayed, for I am your God. I will strengthen you and help you; I will uphold you with my righteous right hand.
Isaiah 41:10

For he will command his angels concerning you to guard you in all your ways.
Psalm 91:11

Fear not, for I have redeemed you; I have summoned you by name; you are mine.
Isaiah 43:1b

_____ ACTS

What courageous acts have you accomplished this week?

What prevents you from carrying on in your courageous journey when you get home?

*Acts of courage are like snapshots ...
Reminders of what Jesus can do through me.*

God on Courage

But whenever you were in distress and turned to the Lord, the God of Israel, and sought him out, you found him.
2 Chronicles 15:4 *(NLT)*

Be strong and courageous. Do not be afraid or terrified because of them, for the LORD your God goes with you; he will never leave you nor forsake you.
Deuteronomy 31:6 *(NIV)*

Don't be intimidated by your enemies.   Philippians 1:28 *(NLT)*

From the LORD comes deliverance.   Psalm 3:8a (NIV)

I can do everything through him [Christ] who gives me strength.
Philippians 4:13 (NIV)

HOPE

People who run away or gradually self-destruct or suddenly end their lives have one thing in common—they feel hopeless. Not just discouraged, but convinced that nothing will end their monotonous, aching pain.

By contrast, the faintest glimmer of hope that things could get better may keep a girl in a lousy romance, may give a boy the courage to forgive another beating from his alcoholic father, may embolden a disheartened teacher to face an insolent class one more morning.

Hope is the battery that jump-starts the human heart. As long as there's hope, we can keep going, keep trying, keep hoping—because hope reproduces hope.

All this is by design, and though we sometimes hope for the wrong thing—that we'll be able to make it on our own or that we can wish a thing undone—hope is what draws us to God. The Apostle Paul talked a lot about hope, declaring that hope will not disappoint us because God is faithful. When the world crashes in on us, he says, "And we know that in all things God works for the good of those who love him, who have been called according to his purpose ...What, then, shall we say in response to this? If God is for us, who can be against us?" Romans 8:28, 31 *(NLT)*.

That's hope—the expectation that there's nothing God can't turn into a miracle of deliverance and help.

What's bothering you right now? Is it bigger than you? Is it bigger than God?

—by Jim Hancock

HOPE WILL NOT DISAPPOINT US BECAUSE GOD IS FAITHFUL.

(adapted from *Good Advice*, Jim Hancock & Todd Temple, Zondervan/Youth Specialties, ©1987)

BE COURAGEOUS AND PUT LOVE INTO ACTION

•Contact all the Christians you can think of to begin a Christian club.

•Carry your Bible to school.

•Write a history paper on Jesus Christ.

•Write a book report on a Christian book.

•Put your favorite Scripture verses or Christian sayings in your locker.

•Write Christian verses and sayings or paste pictures of Christian bands on your book covers.

•Conduct a survey of your classmates' religious beliefs.

•Make name tags or buttons with your club name on them or a provocative statement such as "Ask Me. I Know." This will definitely spark conversations.

•Ask to have your Christian club spotlighted in your school newspaper or television news program.

•Schedule a special music concert for lunch. Invite a church youth choir or a local Christian singer or contemporary band.

•Ask if you can sponsor a special rally promoting sexual abstinence. Invite a local youth pastor or Christian sports figure to speak. Make sure that a student shares about their choice to remain abstinent.

•Visit students who are sick or in the hospital. Pray with them.

•Have a special ice cream or pizza social. Invite everyone. Ask businesses to help sponsor the event financially.

•Give out homemade cookies or brownies at lunch and explain why you are doing it.

•Give out water after school practices for sports teams.

•Invite ten students to a special "What I Think About God" discussion during lunch.

•Pick up trash after school. Let the school administration know you want to help out any way you can.

•Mail Christian birthday cards to your friends.

•Give out Christian Christmas cards to your teachers.

•Sponsor a needy family at Thanksgiving and Christmas and ask your friends to help donate appropriate food and gifts.

•Give treats or candies to all of the teachers at your school with a small note explaining that you are praying for them.

•Put some candy in the teacher's lounge. Next to the candy, put several copies of a thank you letter from your club to the teachers.

•Sit in a different place during lunch and make new friends.

•Invite a new kid to come to the football game.

•During lunch, set up a special "Tutoring Table" and volunteer to tutor students who struggle in their classes.

•Give a sheet of paper or a pencil to anyone who needs one.

•Give someone a ride to school.

•Set up a shuttle system so you can give lots of students rides to school.

•Listen. Listen. Listen.

•Invite friends to your youth group or a Christian concert.

•Meet monthly with other Christian students leading Christian clubs in your city for a time of training and encouragement.

•Start a newsletter to report all that God is doing on campuses all over your city. Distribute it to every church you can find.

GUTSY ACT #6

HAVE COURAGE

Today, I'm committing myself to . . . *(choose one)*

☐
☐ Pray once each hour today* for the person I'm going to share with.

Pray once each hour today* for the person I'm going to share with *and* call this person just to say that I'm thinking about him or her.

☐ Pray once each hour today* for the person I'm going to share with *and* call this person today just to say that I'm thinking about him or her . . .

and commit myself to take a quiet time with Jesus every day next week. *(See Devos, starting on page 73 in this Guidebook for suggested devotional or go to www.livethelife.org.)*

☐ *(write your own Gutsy Act)* _____

_____

_____

_____

_____

SIGN HERE *as confirmation of your commitment.*

_____

*If you have a watch that beeps on the hour, set it to do so. When it beeps, pray!

Keep Practicing

You may be feeling like there is still so much to learn about Living the Life God has called you to live. Guess what? All of us will continue to learn new lessons from God throughout our lives. What we each need to do is exactly what Paul told the Philippians to do. "Whatever you have learned or received or heard from me, or seen in me—put it into practice. And the God of peace will be with you." Philippians 4:9 *(NLT)*

You don't need to wait until you know it all—you never will! Put into practice the lessons God has taught you, and he will continue to teach you and guide you throughout your life!

MEETING 6
LIFE TOGETHER DISCUSSION

Have Courage
Life Together Discussion

1. Refer to page 63. Share how you did in your commitments. What was the toughest part? Will you act on these commitments again today?

2. Name one specific friend you believe God is leading you to share your rescue story with. When, specifically, can you talk with your friend about the need for Jesus to rescue him or her?

3. My greatest fear or concern about talking with my friend is . . . I think that person will react by . . .

4. God might change my friend's life if he or she begins to have a friendship with Jesus by . . .

5. My friendship might change if my friend started to follow Jesus because . . .

6. My life would change if my friend started a relationship with Jesus because . . .

7. Pray together: Say the name of the person you're going to share with, then each of you pray for that person by name. Do this with every person in the group.

Get a GRIP

First Secret: *"The way you live can bring joy to God."*

Get alone with God — Ask him to speak to you . . . listen carefully.

Read God's Word — Ephesians 4:29-5:2. Read it aloud slowly. Listen to what the Holy Spirit wants you to hear.

Investigate and respond — According to this verse, the way you live includes many things. List some of the ways that you could bring *sorrow* to God by the way you live today:

Now list some of the ways that you could live your life today to bring *joy* to God.

Pray about it all! — Ask God to help you today to take one specific action that will bring joy to him. Then talk to him about the areas in which you're afraid you'll stumble. Ask him to lead you *away* from these areas, and to help you to replace these temptations with the good things mentioned in the Ephesians passage.

Today I am committing myself to . . . *(choose one)*

❏ Find a person who I could be tenderhearted toward and do something for that person today.

❏ *Same as above plus* . . . Make a conscious effort to not let any foul or hurtful language come from my mouth.

❏ *Same as above plus* . . . Choose one Christian brother or sister to praise and affirm in a direct, public way.

Remember: In God's mind, you were worth the sacrifice of his only Son. You are his dear child, today and every day.

 **Devos**

Get a GRIP

Second Secret: *"The way I live can honor and please God."*

Get alone with God

Ask him to soften your heart. . . listen carefully.

Read God's Word

Colossians 1:9-14. Read it slowly and aloud. Listen to what the Holy Spirit wants you to hear.

Investigate and respond

On our own, we're not able to live a life that pleases God. To honor and please him, we must first receive his power. Verse 11 mentions two of the results of this power: patience and endurance. Name two areas in your life that could benefit from this kind of patience and endurance:

Why is important for you to know God better and better?

Pray about it all!

Ask God to show you how he sees you today. Then ask him to show you, through this Bible passage, just how important you are to him. (Tip: Writing out your prayers in a special place such as a prayer journal or on your computer may help you to concentrate on your prayers more clearly.)

Today I am committing myself to . . . *(choose one)*

☐ Tell someone the story of my rescue so that I can be reminded of what Jesus rescued me from.

☐ *Same as above plus* . . . Ask that person what he or she believes to be true about Jesus.

☐ *Same as above plus* . . . Pick a person from my family to be the focus of my patience and endurance.

Remember: God rescued you, not because you earned his love in any way. He rescued you because of his deep, unending, unconditional love for you. Because you are his, you will one day share in the awesome inheritance that belongs to all of us who follow him. This can bring you joy!

 **Devos**

Get a GRIP

Third Secret: *"I live to please Jesus instead of living to please myself."*

Get alone with God

Close your eyes and ask Jesus to meet with you in a special, powerful way today.

Read God's Word

2 Corinthians 5:14-21. Read it slowly and write out verses 17, 18, and 19.

Investigate and respond

One of the many ways to please Jesus is to learn to tell others the story of your own rescue—and how this same loving Jesus died to rescue them too. Write down the name of the person you are going to share the gospel with here:

When will you share the good news to this person?

Pray about it all!

Ask Jesus to use his love to control you and your actions. (Tip: This kind of growth takes place in a process—like a journey. Don't expect everything at once. Just ask him to help you grow today—in your love for him and others.) Pray—ask God to use his love to control you and your actions. This kind of growth happens in a process (like a journey), so don't expect to be perfect today. Just ask him to help you to grow in your love for the people around you, for your family and for him.

Today I am committing myself to . . . (*choose one*)

❏ Clearly demonstrate my love for one friend today. Name of friend: _____

❏ *Same as above plus* . . . Tell this friend my rescue story.

❏ *Same as above plus* . . . Ask this friend if there is anything I can be praying for him or her . . . then remember to pray that prayer.

Remember: Whether you feel it or not, you have a new life. This new life is real because Jesus died for you. God has given you the privilege of passing this message on to other people. As you look for opportunities to tell others, let God lead you. He is already at work in your life and in the lives of other people in your world.

 **Get a GRIP**

Fourth Secret: *"If I live in a way that pleases God, others will respect the way I live."*

Get alone with God   Begin by telling him that you love and need him today.

Read God's Word   1 Thessalonians 4:1-12. Read it slowly and aloud. Listen carefully to what the Holy Spirit wants you to hear.

Investigate and respond   Think this one through.

Living in a way that pleases God will involve sexual purity. In this passage, the Lord is telling us to keep clear of all sexual sin. This one area of life can cause any of us to nose dive into a crash landing. What do you need to do to keep clear of sexual sin? What do you need to eliminate from your life today that will help you to live a pure life?

Pray about it all!   Tell God your struggles in this area of life. Ask him to help you to live in a way that pleases him. He is able to listen to your questions and struggles, even about sex.

Today I am committing myself to . . . *(choose one)*

❑   Keep clear of sexual sin by _____

❑ *Same as above plus* . . . Ask a trusted friend to hold me accountable for the sexual area of my life.

❑ *Same as above plus* . . . Ask that friend to pray with me today about this area of life.

Remember: God wants to help you, even in the awkward areas of life. He does not expect you to live a life that pleases him all on your own. He wants to walk on this journey with you every step of the way.

Get a GRIP

Fifth Secret: *"If I carefully listen to God, the Holy Spirit will reveal many things to me."*

Get alone with God Ask God to speak to you today . . . listen carefully.

Read God's Word John 16:12-15. Read it slowly and out loud.

Investigate and respond Over the last four days, what do you think you have heard from God?

Pray about it all! Ask God to help you to follow through with the commitments that you have made. Ask him to give you all that you will need in order to follow him and do what he has asked you to do.

Today I am committing myself to . . . *(choose one)*

☐ Listen carefully to the Lord throughout this day, expecting him to speak to me.

☐ *Same as above plus* . . . Tell a trusted Christian friend what I think God has been saying to me.

☐ *Same as above plus* . . . Pray with that friend and allow for a few minutes of silence so that God can speak to both of us.

Remember: God wants to reveal important things to you because you are his child and his friend. Spending time waiting to hear from him is a part of prayer that is worth practicing.

 **Get a GRIP**

Sixth Secret: *"As I Live the Life, others will realize that they can trust Jesus and receive eternal life."*

Get alone with God   Ask God to remind you of the kindness and patience that he has shown to you.

Read God's Word   1 Timothy 1:14-17. Read it slowly and aloud.

Investigate and respond   You know this stuff, but it sure helps to be reminded . . . Jesus came to rescue us from our sin and death and from a life without him. He came to save even the worst of us. He has been so patient with you. Now he wants to use you as an example of someone who has been rescued. He wants to use you as his messenger to the people in your life who do not yet have a relationship with him. They need him as much as you need him. Now—What friend in your life needs Jesus?

List three possible ways that you could show this person how loving and patient Jesus is.

Pray about it all!   Ask God to work in the life of the person who you want to see come into a relationship with God. Ask him to show you what you could do today to reach out in love to your friend.

Today I am committing myself to . . . *(choose one)*

❑ Pray regularly for my friend who needs Jesus.

❑ *Same as above plus* . . . Share my rescue story with this friend.

❑ *Same as above plus* . . . Ask them where they see themselves in relation to Jesus and explain the incredible message of Jesus' death and resurrection and what that could mean for them. I will ask them if they are ready to entrust their life to Jesus.

Remember: God's mercy in your life is some of the best evidence that you have for the truth of your faith. As you explain your story and his story, be patient with your friend's response. God is already at work in their life. You do not have to force them into their journey with Jesus.

Get a GRIP

Seventh Secret: *"By using the Psalms, I can give praise and thanks to God every day."*

Get alone with God   Ask God to meet you today in a unique way . . . watch for his presence and listen for his voice all day long, not just in this devotional time.

Read God's Word   Psalm 103. Read it aloud—slowly.

Investigate and respond   Answer this one—Using this passage, make a list of all the reasons that you have to praise God:

Circle the three things about God that are most important to you today.

Pray about it all!   Go back through your list and express those things to God in your own words, in a personal way. Thank him and praise him for the good things he does for you (verses 2 and 5)

Today I am committing myself to . . . *(choose one)*

☐   Continue to have a "Get a GRIP" time (or similar devotional time) with God for the next seven days.

☐ *Same as above plus* . . . Continue to have a "Get a GRIP" time (or similar devotional time) with God for the next month.

Remember: God's love for you is unfailing: He will never leave you. You are his precious child. He understands you, even better than you understand yourself. He considers you to be his friend.

DIGGING DEEPER

The values in each of the Live the Life lessons all come from God's Word. Here are some additional verses that we did not talk about during the training, but that are at the foundation of everything you've been learning.

DEPEND ON JESUS

For there is one God and one mediator between God and men, the man Christ Jesus, who gave himself as a ransom for all men--the testimony given in its proper time.
1 Timothy 2:5-6

For all have sinned and fall short of the glory of God.
Romans 3:23

If you love me, you will obey what I command.
John 14:15

Here I am! I stand at the door and knock. If anyone hears my voice and opens the door, I will come in and eat with him, and he with me.
Revelation 3:20

Unless the LORD builds the house, its builders labor in vain. Unless the LORD watches over the city, the watchmen stand guard in vain.
Psalm 127:1

BE REAL

This is the message we have heard from him and declare to you: God is light; in him there is no darkness at all. If we claim to have fellowship with him yet walk in the darkness, we lie and do not live by the truth. But if we walk in the light, as he is in the light, we have fellowship with one another, and the blood of Jesus, his Son, purifies us from all sin. If we claim to be without sin, we deceive ourselves and the truth is not in us. If we confess our sins, he is faithful and just and will forgive us our sins and purify us from all unrighteousness.
1 John 1:5-9

Therefore confess your sins to each other and pray for each other so that you may be healed. The prayer of a righteous man is powerful and effective.
James 5:16

SHARE THE GOSPEL

But in your hearts set apart Christ as Lord. Always be prepared to give an answer to everyone who asks you to give the reason for the hope that you have. But do this with gentleness and respect.
Peter 3:15

GET CONNECTED

They devoted themselves to the apostles' teaching and to the fellowship, to the breaking of bread and to prayer. Everyone was filled with awe, and many wonders and miraculous signs were done by the apostles. All the believers were together and had everything in common. Selling their possessions and goods, they gave to anyone as he had need. Every day they continued to meet together in the temple courts. They broke bread in their homes and ate together with glad and sincere hearts, praising God and enjoying the favor of all the people. And the Lord added to their number daily those who were being saved.
Acts 2:42-47

A friend loves at all times, and a brother is born for adversity.
Proverbs 17:17

Therefore each of you must put off falsehood and speak truthfully to his neighbor, for we are all members of one body.
Ephesians 4:25

HAVE COURAGE

I am not ashamed of the gospel, because it is the power of God for the salvation of everyone who believes: first for the Jew, then for the Gentile.
Romans 1:16

But every spirit that does not acknowledge Jesus is not from God. This is the spirit of the antichrist, which you have heard is coming and even now is already in the world.
1 John 4:3

STUDENT SPIRITUAL LIFE RESOURCES

There's so much more good stuff we want to tell you about, but we're out of pages and out of time. So, here's a list of books, devotionals, and other materials that can help you out. See page 80 for phone numbers and Web addresses to all these publishers

BIBLES

• *Student's Life Application Bible*—New Living Translation. (Tyndale)

• *New Believer's Bible* (NLT)—Great gift for new Christians. (Tyndale)

• *The New Student Bible*—New International Version (Zondervan)

PERSONAL DEVOTIONALS

• *Just Between God and You*—a 28-day journal designed to guide you into a personal encounter with God. (Youth for Christ)

• *Youthwalk* (Walk Thru the Bible)

• *Freedom in Christ for Teens Devotionals* by Neil Anderson and DavePark (Harvest)

• *Wild Truth Journal for Junior Highers* (Youth Specialties)

• *Grow For It! Journal* (Youth Specialties)

• *Grow For It! Journal through the Scriptures* (Youth Specialties)

• *WWJD Spiritual Challenge Journal* (Youth Specialties)

• *Wild Truth Journal by Mark Oestreicher* (Youth Specialties/10 TO 20 Press)

EVANGELISM TOOLS

• *LIFE: Lessons in Friendship Evangelism*—Learn about sharing your faith, lovingothers, praying, and making disciples. (Youth for Christ)

- *Life's Greatest Adventure*—Here's a great tool to help you live to tell. These booklets help you share Life's Greatest Adventure with your friends. (Youth for Christ)

- *Life Band Witness Bracelet*—A witness tool that incorporates both the visual concept of the salvation plan along with the printed word. The complete package includes a leather bracelet with five colored beads, *Life's Greatest Adventure* booklet, and a teaching tool to share the gospel using this Life Band. (Youth for Christ)

FOLLOW-UP MATERIALS

- *Totally True*—Six lessons teaching the important basics of the Christian life. (Youth for Christ)

- *Life's Growing Adventure*—A 14-day study for new Christians. (Youth for Christ)

- *Wake Up Call*—In this four-part video series, Richard K. Allison uses his dramatic skills to help you know God better. (Youth for Christ)

- *Journey Backpack*—This leather-bottom backpack contains the *Student's Life Application Bible (New Living Translation)*, the Bible on CD-ROM *(NLT)*, *Jumper Fables* by Ken Davis, a prayer journal with study notes by Bill Hybels, evangelism resources, and other materials. (Youth for Christ)

EVANGELISM TRAINING

- *Live to Tell*—This interactive video curriculum is from DC/LA '94. Each set comes with 2 VHS tapes (3 sessions on each tape) and a Leader's Guide. (Youth for Christ)

DISCUSSION STARTERS

Use these resources in student-led campus clubs:

- *Discussion & Lesson Starters* (Youth Specialties)

- *Discussion & Lessons Starters 2* (Youth Specialties)

- *High School TalkSheets* (Youth Specialties)

- *High School TalkSheets: Psalms and Proverbs* (Youth Specialties)

- *More High School TalkSheets* (Youth Specialties)

- EdgeTV has one mission: to create a safe place to talk about unsafe things. No easy answers. No short cuts. No lie. Guaranteed. For more information or to order these videos call IMS Productions at 800-616-EDGE.

- 10 TO 20 produces video, multimedia, live-media programming for conferences and special events, and some quirky-cool books for teenagers. 10 TO 20 • P.O. Box 604 Del Mar, CA 92014 • 619-793-8275 •10to20@compuserve.com

ADDITIONAL RESOURCES TO READ

- *Can I Be a Christian without Being Weird?* by Kevin Johnson (Bethany)

- *Don't Check Your Brains at the Door* by Josh McDowell and Bob Hostetler (Word)

- *How to Give Away Your Faith* by Paul Little (InterVarsity)

- *Keeping Your Cool While Sharing Your Faith* by Greg Johnson and Susie Shellenberger (Tyndale)

- *Know Why You Believe* by Paul Little (NavPress)

- *Leading the Way* by Paul Borthwick (NavPress)

- *Mere Christianity* by C.S. Lewis (Simon & Schuster)

- *More Than a Carpenter* by Josh McDowell (Tyndale)

- *My Heart, Christ's Home* by Robert Boyd Munger (InterVarsity)

- *To My Dear Slimeball* by Rich Miller (Harvest)

- *Under Siege* by Josh McDowell and Chuck Klein (Word)

Bethany House
www.bethanyhouse.com
800-328-6109

Harvest House
888-501-6991

InterVarsity Press
www.gospelcom.net/ivp
630-887-2500

NavPress
www.navpress.org
800-366-7788

Simon & Schuster
www.simonsays.com
800-223-2336

Tyndale House
www.tyndale.com
800-323-9400

Walk Thru the Bible
www.walkthru.org
800-763-5433

Word Publishing
www.thomasnelson.com
800-933-9673

Youth for Christ
www.livethelife.org
www.shopyfc.org
800-735-3252

Youth Specialties
www.YouthSpecialties.com
800-776-8008

Zondervan
www.zondervan.com
800-727-1309

CAMPUS CLUB RESOURCES

- Campus Journal—a free resource! RBC Ministries www.gospelcom.net/rbs/cj 800-598-7221

- Meeting the Equal Access Challenge—knowing your rights as a Christian in a public school. (Youth for Christ)

- *12-Minute Meetings for Campus Christian Clubs*—40 complete student-led meetings for Bible clubs. Also, *More 12-Minute Meetings for Campus Christian Clubs* and *Still More 12-Minute Meetings for Campus Christian Clubs* (40 meetings each). Youth Alive • 1445 Boonville, MO 65802 800-545-2766.

- For the handbook *Student's Legal Rights* by J.W. Brinkley contact Roever Communicationswww.interplaza.com/roever P.O. Box 136130 • Ft. Worth, TX 76136 • 817-238-2000

- For information on creation versus evolution contact Institute for Creation Research • www.icr.org • P.O. Box 2667 El Cajon, CA 92021-0667 • 619-448-0900

CAMPUS CLUB LEGAL INFORMATION

Legal counsel can be obtained from the following organizations:

- Christian Legal Society • www.clsnet.com • 4208 Evergreen Lane • Suite 222 • Annandale, VA 22003-3264 • 703-642-1070

- Citizens for Excellence in Education • www.nace-cee.org • P.O. Box 3200 • Costa Mesa, CA 92628 • 949-251-9333

- National Legal Foundation • www.nlf.net • P.O. Box D • Chesapeake, VA 23328-0004 • 757-424-4242

- Rutherford Institute • www.rutherford.org • P.O. Box 7482 • Charlottesville, VA 22906-7482 • 804-978-3888

- The American Center for Law and Justice • P.O. Box 450349 Atlanta, GA 31145 • 404-320-6870

- Eagle Forum • www.eagleforum.org • P.O. Box 618 • Alton, IL 62002 • 618-462-5415

NOTES

NOTES

NOTES

NOTES

NOTES

NOTES

NOTES

Where to find stuff in this Guidebook you really liked